EXpressIon

Meagan Torrez

I CORINTHIANS 13:13

AND NOW ABIDETH FAITH, HOPE, CHARITY, THESE THREE; BUT THE GREATEST OF THESE IS CHARITY.

Acknowledgements

I would like to thank God for his grace and mercy. A special thank you to my daughter Kirsten Sanaa and son Ezekiel Nicanor for being my motivation and joy. I want to thank my husband Jerry Torrez for his continual love and support. As well as my family, the Gooden's, for always helping me grow and push forward. Special thanks to the Moultrie, Pannell, Singleton, and Keeton families for years of wisdom and support.

Love You.

CONTENTS

NAKED TRUTH

ILL BE BACK IN THE MORNING

SOLD OUT

WASTED LOVE

HOPE

THE PROPOSAL

JUSTICE WILL TRIUMPH

SISTERS KEEPER

BAD COLOGNE

SALVATION ARMY

THERES POWER IN SUBMISSION

WHO INVITED GRACE?

SINNERS PERCEPTION

LITTLE GIRL

GOD

WILL

NOT

STOP

THE

STORM

UNTIL

YOU

SEE

HIM

IN

IT

Naked

Truth

STRIP! Take it off. Piece by piece. Mind off carnal things, I'm talking about those leaves.

Having used to cover shame. Time to reorganize the experience, value the moment, mistakes own it.

It's not a true testimony until you're not ashamed to tell it.

These are the cards that were played.

The devil cut the deck, but I was the one that dealt it.

No need for me to be naked and ashamed, Jesus took the blame.

So ill talk about that pain that tried to leave a stain.

Wanted my love to teach me and protect me.

As I grew up, she would always reject me, which would always upset me.

I would get close to her; she would push me away.

Saying Meagan, I'm tired, telling me to go play.

So, I played.

Where the devil stayed.

My best friend's father was molesting his daughters.

My best friend was touching on me.

Since the age of thirteen I haven't really been able to sleep.

I was afraid of the dark because I would wake up with demons choking me.

They would breathe and laugh in my face.

When I would awake my body would ache.

I've been through the heartbreak.

I fell in love before, when God is not in it, the devil has an open door.

He had my heart, but his heart was in the sheets.

Great woman but my wo wasn't enough for him so with transsexuals he use to creep.

Been through the heartache.

I had this secret love that was more like a drug.

My heart he would invade, then betray.

The devil plays in the dark you see so that secret we had to keep my heart was more like his slave.

One thing about pain, it will leave when you let it go.

So that secret we had to keep.

I don't keep it anymore.

Most of the time when people saw me, I was laughing and playing.

Nobody knew about the secret pain.

I had the devil two stepping on my brain.

Contemplated suicide.

Not many people knew it.

That was something that I tried.

First taste of alcohol at the age of six

Ever since alcohol has been my bliss.

So just because the cups from Chick fil a doesn't mean its lemonade.

Gin and juice were my best friend.

Little coke don't forget the Henn.

Special cognac never blend in.

Walking up and down ABC liquor looking for that best friend.

Smoking until I'm choking.

Inhale until I can't breathe.

Exhale but keep smoking to make sure my high doesn't leave.

I've been shot at by the police.

Been to Afghanistan twice.

Rockets flying over my head so close, I can feel the heat.

Suicide bomber standing near, as a matter of fact ten feet.

I've been through the depression, oppression, rejection, and neglection.

But I stand here healed now because of Christ affection.

Standing on my past and the devil as a testimony to come up a little higher in God.

Knowing whatever comes whatever that may be, beautiful by the morning my life shall be.

My morning doesn't come with the sun, my morning has come because of Gods Son.

My morning is He.

Product of His amazing grace because of the master's peace I am a masterpiece.

True work of art because believe.

So, I step back and let God flow.

Take his will and let mine go!

Fighting the devil with this necessary evil.

This is my truth moment.

My sweetest revenge.

Wait get my good side follow me as I follow Christ.

My new best friend.

WHEN

YOU

HANDLE

GODS

BUSINESS

HE

WILL

HANDLE

YOURS

I'll Be Back

In The Morning

Why doesn't my first love love me back?

I'm addicted to his touch therefore addicted to his lust.

So fine to me, what a sight to see.

Addicted to his taste the way he handles my waist. He holds me strong.

When I'm with him I can only do wrong.

Doing things in secret but it can't be hidden let's face it I'm sinning.

Why does fruit taste so good when it's forbidden?

I love the sensation of giving into my temptation.

Gods wondering where I am because when I'm in sin I'm gone from him.

Seeking after the fruit that's in the midst of the garden, trying to finish what the devil started.

Ye shall not eat of it, neither shall ye touch it, lest ye die.

You want me to just look at that and walk right by? When it comes to sin, I'm not shy.

Seduction is in my eye, lust of the eyes, lust of the flesh, and the pride of life.

When it comes to this fruit I have the devil's appetite, don't always want the Christian life. God says don't love the world. It's hard when our first love was sin.

He speaks to me in a seductive tone, lusting the way he leads me on,

   I can only have one husband.

War in my members, inside there's a fight going on.

Every day he flirts with me, trying to attract me to finish this love affair.

I'm in so deep now, I don't even care if the people stare.

Got married, but sometimes I feel like I'm being ignored and the attention I crave the one from my past gives me more and more.

I lift my hands in church but when my ex comes around, I flirt.

My husband loves me dearly, he gave his only Son for me.

I don't know why I cheat. It's usually in the nighttime when I think he's asleep.

Weeping may endure for a night; well, I'll be back in the morning.

Addicted to the night life but when you're in the dark, good and evil look alike.

See darkness can't exist in the presence of light.

So, if I think on dead things, dead things I will be. Until I truly receive His life, He cannot resurrect me.

Buried alive, no one can hear my cry. How can it be time for me to die when I have yet to live life?

Refusing to tell hell, no, flesh I didn't want to let go.

My first love dropped me so deep; it feels like I'm six feet.

But sins power is broken over me, if I continue there in, true life, I'm playing pretend.

Does your husband know you're lonely?

Me thinking, when I was with my first love it wasn't good while it lasted, so why do I sit here thinking about how I wish time wouldn't have passed?

Being that he was my first, a new love is hard to begin, my desire was to be with sin. Even though time was a waste, I noticed, my ex never wanted commitment all he wanted to do was fornicate.

How can me and my husband build this relationship if I keep going on these cheap dates? Jesus knew no sin so when I'm in sin me and Him cannot relate.

Like Mary at a tomb looking for my savior, thinking for me there is no hope.

Woman why weepest thou whom seekest thou? He went up a little higher so my sins could have a cloak.

Remembering to marry me He had blood dripping from His hands and feet.

If I continue in sin, I can't claim to belong to Him.

I can no longer take this marriage for granted.

No longer in lust with God rather in love. I thought sin was someone I could call my lover, but sin is just a luster.

I wrote this suicidal letter to sin to tell him I'm dying within, and you can't have me anymore. My Husband paid a cost for me that you cannot afford.

For of the abundance of the heart the mouth speaks. The lip of truth shall be established forever.

As a man thinketh in his heart so is he. Where am I going with this? Romans 10, a place where you too can be free. Redemption is closer than it seems. With your own heart and mouth confess and believe.

Born of a virgin, died for our sins, blood shed on the cross, resurrected the third day. Released from the penalty, His love is a privilege.

This is the foundation of our faith.

Our Father's desire is that His children's souls are saved and have life beyond the grave.

LOOK

 FOR

GOD

IN

EVERY

SITUATION

Sold Out

We pick up our cross.

We die daily.

I challenge you to compare your death walk to the last seven words of Jesus on the cross.

Transforming to transitioning to transcending.

Father forgive them for they know not what they do.

Which is love for the brethren.

To speak well of my enemy is to speak well of you.

My life is not my own therefore they are not trespassing against me but against Thee

So, to sin in ignorance is one thing but to sin and know the truth.

That's a greater sin for you.

Transforming to transitioning to transcending

Verily I say unto thee, today shall thou be with me in paradise.

Repentant hearts promise.

But we are forever judging the brother to left.

Only accepting ones that have the same mental disorder as me.

Forgetting all our minds need to be renewed.

Don't accept our brothers and sisters but want God to accept you.

We are to bare the infirmities of the weak.

Paradise wasn't a promise to the righteous but to ones that see they were sinners just like me.

Can't judge because we don't sin like you.

Comes a time we must look these religious bullies in the face.

OUR FATHER, hallowed be thy name

He's my God too.

Transforming to transitioning to transcending.

Behold thy son! Behold thy mother!

Family

We have received the spirit of adoption whereby we cry Abba Father

Who is my mother? Our my brethren?

He that does the will of the father.

For the servant knoweth not what his lord doeth.

For I have called you friend.

But there is a friend that sticketh closer than a brother.

Transforming to transitioning to transcending.

My God My God Why hast thou forsaken me.

Sometimes it feels like God is not around.

Feeling anguish and pain

That spiritual separation from the name

But I will never leave thee nor forsake thee.

Keep pressing toward the aim.

Transforming to transitioning to transcending.

I thirst.

They gave me gall for my meat and in my thirst, they gave me vinegar to drink.

Didn't quench his thirst until his suffering was over for me.

Man shall not live by bread alone.

My meat is to do the will of him that sent me.

All I live by, all I live by, all I live by, is his tone.

Transforming to transitioning to transcending.

It is finish.

Pressing toward the end.

Not looking back to sin.

He will finish the work he has placed within.

Refusing the hyssop for now not taking the easy way out.

Not a forgetful hearer but a doer of the work.

Keep myself unspotted from the world.

Bridle my tongue.

Visit fatherless and widows not when they are good but afflicted and misunderstood.

Transforming to transitioning to transcending.

Father into thy hands I commend my spirit.

Sometimes it feels Gods plan is not working and I want to do me.

But I die daily put myself on the alter.

Burn my flesh up.

Lord, I sacrifice me.

Giving up the ghost for the Holy Ghost

Realizing what matters most.

Romans 12:1 Be ye transformed by the renewing of your mind.

Until we serve God right mentally, we can't serve God righteously physically.

How are you living?

Sold out continually giving God a nevertheless or a sellout.

Making excuses for your sinning covering it up with religion.

Shake the religion off and pick up your cross

Bought with a price he purchased our life.

Chosen generation.

We shall live sold out to Christ.

COMMUNICATE

LIKE

JESUS

Wasted Love

What manner of love the father has bestowed

What he has given is nothing that was owed.

Putting away the old walking in the new

Many are called but he made you one of the few

Could it be! Finally! someone to love me.

That's too good to be true.

What if he does me like all the others do?

Rejected when all I wanted was acceptance.

Rejected by this world, that's not where you belong.

You belong in the master's arms.

God created you to be a new creature with his features.

Let him and not the world be your teacher.

Don't be one that only receives the level of love you allow yourself to believe.

Hiding behind your hurt

Not realizing who loved you first.

God's love fulfills and keeps you from the devils lies.

Where whatever's wrong feels right

Carnal things only pacify it never satisfies.

I'm not here to offer you religion.

I'm here to offer you repentance.

To no longer seek to cover your sins more than you cover your spirit.

Not an experiment but an experience.

Teach you a new *expression* where we *EX I* and *PRESS ON* until poverty is gone.

Not the poverty in the recession, the poverty in your spirit.

He that has an ear to hear, I pray you hear it.

Can you hear me now?

Because death is deaf.

Therefore, my sheep know my voice.

No longer do you have to have your confidence in this world insecurities.

No longer in the worlds love.

How can the world teach you about something it did not create?

The world tries to make love.

But love has already been made.

Not Buddha not Muhammed but when Jesus Christ got up from the grave.

That's why roses die, bubble baths get cold, chocolate covered strawberries get mold. What you are used to calling love gets old.

He is an eternal God.

So, if God is not the foundation and love is not the motivation it will not last.

How can you grab your future if you don't first let go of your past?

I know nothing motivates you like the last minute.

What if you don't know when the last minute is?

He's coming like a thief in the night, a twinkling of an eye were going up to heaven.

Trying to teach you not to seek to be one of the twelve but to seek to be one of the eleven.

Let him hide you behind the cross

He already paid the cost.

Please don't be his child and remain lost.

It would be ashamed to be a sanctified atheist.

To be offered this love and not want to taste it.

And that one day when God says to you.

What did you do with my love?

You say.

I wasted it.

LOVE

HOPE

FAITH

Hope

I've been trying to get to know you.

You keep rejecting me.

Speaking life to you because you are already delivered.

Crying on the inside

I am one of the first to hear, giving you greater reason to live.

I am the enemy of your depression.

You tried to quit.

I wouldn't let you go.

When will you realize?

You must be patient with me. I told you I was coming.

I am still one you can turn to.

The one you can give your all.

Wiping your tears keeping them from the slow drip that continually falls,

Down your face.

I am trying to explain to you I am one you can hold on to.

When it comes to you, I have a tight grip.

You've looked for me in family, still fail to fine.

Looked for me in men couldn't find me in a perfect ten.

Looked for me in women on none you could depend on or find that true friend

Looked to the left thought no one was there except self.

Looked to the right, it was me there holding you tight.

Looking around at all the people, feeling no one was there to call your equal.

Went from looking up to looking down, until it was me you found.

The one that wiped your tears and helped you face your fears.

Scared at night it was me that held your hand tight.

When you wanted to fight it was me that calmed you down until you got right

Telling you to give yourself a hug when you felt you lacked love.

Head down it was me that lifted it up.

When you fell it was me that picked you up.

Dedicated to keep you motivated to keep trying again and again.

I do not associate with those that forget God therefore I remind you of his word so in your heart there is a complete aw.

I am your friend, your lover, I am there when you think you can't find another.

I am close friends with strength and the father's tone, I never come alone.

I am the push in your back.

The movement in your feet when you feel you want to slack.

The cure for breast cancer making life a little fancier.

A true friend in your marriage.

I was there when you had that miscarriage.

Your confident expectation

Has the building of your room been impoverished with bitterness and hopelessness?

I AM HOPE

THE PROPOSAL

Kings and Queens, Kings and Queens.

What God has joined together let no man put asunder.

Not even, YOU TWO, have become one flesh.

With one faith, one Lord, one baptism.

These three are one.

You can't do this without the Father, the Son,

Filling you with the Holy Ghost.

Desire a spouse God given. Jesus married the church.

Now let's see what kind of spouse you think you're worth.

This is a test; you can't love her right until every area of your heart surrenders to Christ.

Please be patient, be kind, no envy, boast, nor pride, rudeness, neither self-seeking eyes.

Not easily angered, get to know each other daily as if you were strangers.

No records of wrongs, seventy times seven.

Mr. and Mrs. Perfect do not exist.

He is a God that pardons.

Ready to forgive.

Delight not in evil, rejoice in truth, be of good use.

Too much substance, to allow a carnal mentality to keep.

 interrupting what you're chosen to do.

More fish in the sea, that's dirty water, be faithful to each

other.

Many people don't commit, not wanting to submit to

higher power.

 Boldness, humility, faith, it takes, to cherish a heart and

 not break.

It exposes you.

You! The most vulnerable you.

Strip! Take it off piece by piece, mind off carnal things, I'm

 talking about those leaves, leave mother, father, cleave.

His mother stood by as he cleaved to the cross

Love is precious, you know the cost.

This is a place our debt to him is embraced.

Yeshua loves the church. Don't talk about his wife unless

 you're ready to reveal your dirt.

Model the way God relates to His people.

Compliment his presence, keep His presence essence.

God is foundation, love is motivation.

The world cannot teach you marriage.

The world did not create it.

Roses die, bubble baths get cold, chocolate covered

 strawberries get mold.

So be the man in Romance.

By taking His hand, following His plan, take a stand and His

 land.

This ground is holy.

A sacred thing.

The world has corrupted this thing, don't consider it

 strange though when Yeshua comes back for his rainbow.

Love, the expression of God, so EX I and PRESS ON

Die to yourself.

For love is strong as death

It cannot be killed by time or disaster.

Love is gift in action.

Shared within guidelines where God is master.

Rely on each other, Keep no secrets.

Practice love not feelings

Man is separated from God by his desire to act on his own.

Man! Creation! You may fall.

If you switch the order from which you were called.

Know your assignment. Stay the course.

Focus on marriage, Not divorce.

Don't argue with her, she's always right.

You will not win that fight.

God gets the last word of every argument.

Stick to the scriptures, He doesn't care who started it.

When he believes, Help his unbelief.

HELP! When pressure is too heavy because there's a shift.

Be about your father's business. Build His house, YOU

won't always get it right. Keep repenting.

Inhale His breath, Exhale His death.

That he breathed into your nostrils.

Made in His image. Remember your linage.

Love is accepted not earned. So, love without caution.

Marriage! Oath sworn before God.

Any violation of this covenant invites Gods judgment.

Lord loves loyalty.

Remember His royalty.

When the trumpet blows. He's coming Back for His bride.

Be sure to have yours with no more leaves to hide.

SUPERMAN

CAN'T

SAVE

YOU

JUSTICE WILL TRIUMPH

Free at last, Free at last, Thank God all mighty we are free at last.

Take me there, till justice has triumphed.

To the courageous Mrs. Parks refusing her seat.

Take me there, when Dr. King had that speech, telling my dreams to leap.

Take me there, to when El Hajj Malik El Shabazz said, "I'm for truth no matter who tells it, I'm for justice no matter who it is for or against."

I won't sit and dwell on the past. But I refuse to act as if the significant of black has not had an affect that didn't last.

Convictions are from truth not my expression of opinion.

I will not force you to adhere to my stipulation. Neither am I here for your amazement.

Varied opinions on issues but stay unified. Black being beautiful needs to be clarified.

"Deciding to stick with love, hate is too great a burden to bear." But you hate me, don't you? Walk pass me, won't speak. Treat me as if the statue of liberty is no kin to me.

You want me to look upon the American eagle and think I could never take that leap.

Why you want to fly black bird? You aint ever gonna fly, as if a winner is not me. A winner is a dreamer who never gives up. Mandela helps me to stay on my feet.

Mounting up with wings as eagles. Respect for all Gods people.

"Trying not to be judged by the color of my skin but the content of my character." Daddy what color are we? We black girl! But it was my Caucasian great grandfather who raped my Indian great grandmother which gave me this color,

Can I touch your hair? Call my hair nappy and I'll take you to the root of it. Strength, Glory, the truth of it. The creator he numbered it spoke growth and loves it.

You can't hate the root of the tree and not hate the tree. Treated as if black is a prison to me. Who taught you to hate yourself.

Black women and their attitudes. A land that won't defend you, what would you do? They are so loud. Yet no one hears you.

Caked up in makeup, masked in mascara. Full of foundation. Where is your foundation? Walking around as if chains are still a part of your transportation.

Cruising down the street in my six fo. Radio turned up. All they play is what's negative and corrupt.

There go the police. Do you know why I pulled you over? Being black on a Friday night. I answered. It's a black out trying to take the blackout, mental illness is what they blame now. When racism is your idol who's going to take the blame now?

Mad because Ariel is black now. Wait until you meet Jesus, you really going to want to call ICE now! FAITH, we sought your face, suffering seems in vain now.

But just do what they say, I can't breathe. By any means, necessary. X wasn't teaching violence he was saying defend me. A little police brutality. Justice will triumph over this legally blind mentality.

See you less than MAN. DELA. Education is the most powerful weapon. But I thought he had a gun. Educated black man is a dangerous threat. Kept us out of good schools then called us ignorant. My people are destroyed by a lack of knowledge. Look at that disfigurement. Don't leave you mind in Africa. One thousand slaves freed. Tubman. Would have freed one thousand more if they knew they were slaves. Get money still buy chains.

You dropped your crown. Martin told you; you were king. In God we trust. What if the brother doesn't look like us. Hang my brother, while my brother's grandmother hangs a portrait of white jesus without Yeshua's features.

The ox knoweth his owner and the ass his master's crib. But Israel doth not know my people doth not consider. Not man, not money but YHWH is your deliverer. If it's a white man's religion. Jesus would have been white in the scriptures. Yeshua is still that Moses in the river. Come to the forgiver.

Ye are the salt but don't be that pillar. Looking back. Going away backward Continuing to sin. Cutting yourself from Gods help. His hands not too short to save. It's still not withered. Justice will triumph. Only a matter of time that snake can slither.

BE

GREAT

 AT

HOME

FIRST

SISTERS
KEEPER

When it comes to being a woman, do you judge me?

I don't like to wear a dress.

Don't wear my skirts with a high split.

Put on heels then realize, I can't walk in this.

Do you judge me?

I don't walk with a twist or always cross my legs when I sit.

I don't show cleavage or breast.

Are you offended that I would rather you know me before you knew my flesh?

Cain, are you scared if I raise my standard, your standard you might have to fight?

What the world defines a woman to be is not alright

Do you judge me? I don't wear church hats or dresses down to my ankles.

I don't have my tongues memorized nor a signature shout.

Do you judge me?

Because this is not what a woman is

This is what the world created her to be.

Primping before a mirror chasing latest fashions

Look pass your flesh to realize you're blessed.

A virtuous woman's appearance was never mentioned.

The world said a woman was this.

How can the world know what a woman is when God created her bliss?

Hurt heart.

Now instead of building your house you've built walls.

Write your feelings down so you can put your feelings down.

Leave it in your devotion.

The peace of God shall rule not your emotions.

Talking about your pain

Intoxicating me with who you blame

I can't even walk.

Your heart is blocked, and I keep running into walls.

Leading lady you can't lead behind walls.

You are a woman due to your reverence to God.

Greater faith so he can give you a greater taste.

Naomi bitterness you no longer have to embrace.

Why is it when it comes to being a sister keeper, we get that Hagar spirit and flee

Mind not having the capacity to love pass flaws.

Fine as wine but bitter, Rachels life you should consider.

Keep your heart pure.

To know Him and the power of His resurrection, there should be a continual confession.

Take your hand off the will.

He's the potter, be still.

Jezebel, you can no longer be controlling.

Seek the masters will.

Kissing God not in the right way

Judas, instead of kissing his feet we're in his face.

What can you do for me?

Asking for high things to cover up what insecurity brings.

No longer living life waiting on Rebekah's proposal.

Living life as Leah, weary from wanting man's acceptance.

As if God being husband, wasn't a good enough blessing.

Many lovers not knowing how to accept the righteous water.

Woman caught in adultery.

Baby out of wedlock but the man gets away.

Single parent but its ok

Hosea has a place for you to lay.

Wives treat your husband right.

There's power in submission.

Ask Mary, yielding to the lord.

Be it unto me according to thy word.

Elisabeth

When he speaks my belly leaps

Pregnant with his destiny

And no, I don't worship the ground you walk on

But I will wash your feet while I worship the king.

Ill cook for you

Father gives us our daily bread.

Feeding you what the master says

Woman to woman I am my sister's keeper.

Encourage your sisters, keep her, don't allow this life to defeat her.

PUT

GOD

FIRST

Bad Cologne

I repent! For all these years wasting Gods glory

Trying to get to know his story, ignoring the history and the present.

GOD IS NOT A MAN

He is one that creates but there was a void I was trying to shake.

Struggled with loneliness.

Trying to fill the void with the world's toys.

Too much pride in my eyes to see life is only complete when Jesus is the first, I seek.

Wanting the world to care like God cared got me nowhere.

Two is better than one.

I used to seek that instead of Gods Son

Seeking after Gods beautiful creation

Due to the fact man was made from dust I only found frustration.

When you seek things without putting God first at the end of the day you will only feed your hurt

That love that could have been good ends up being more like a curse.

Man was made to manage, to man was given to rule and have dominion.

Seeking after man and what I thought was manly.

Now that man wears skinny jeans that man failed me.

Made in Gods image but I let the world dress me and thought I was sharp.

Refusing to raise the standard and not blend in

Scared I would have to walk alone and not have the world for a friend.

Let's face it I settled.

It was me and the world sitting in a tree.

K I S S I N G,

First comes lust of the eyes, then comes lust of the flesh, then comes the pride of life, then comes the devil's appetite.

I was in love with the world.

From the smile to the frown long as I had the world it didn't matter if we were up or down

Until God got in the way of my world and that world left me

Cried

But the tears were ignored because this world could not afford.

World couldn't heal my cry because the world was a guy.

When you struggle to believe you struggle to perceive

I couldn't see that man could not complete me.

Like Eve carnal things couldn't satisfy my spirit

Big muscles could pick me up in the natural, not in my spirit.

Still waiting on Adam to speak while Eve is being deceived.

With death I would cleave, covering myself with leaves

When God saw me, it left him bereaved.

Until I saw him for myself and believed

I conquered loneliness when I realized it was ok for me to be there for myself.

Stop seeking man and seek Gods help.

Matthew 2:11

When they saw Him, they fell down and worshiped.

Until I saw him for who he really is

The world caused me tears.

How long will you mourn over Saul?

Seeing I have rejected him.

Jesus fully divine fully man I've accepted Him.

FOLLOW

PEACE

SALVATION ARMY

This is a war zone. Comms not clear, I can't hear, His tone. Shadow of death, no evil will, I fear. Thou shalt not kill, obeying the sixth, general order eleven at risk.

To be especially watchful at night and during the time for challenging, to challenge all persons on or near my post, and to allow no one to past without proper authority.

Its dark. I spot movement on the gate. Mind is running like Onesismus. Runaway slave. Proper protocol before the blast. Five, locked and loaded. Safety off. Kill or be killed. The motto we live. Four, God I don't want to kill this man. Three, Deaths about to be revealed. Two, Last warning, get down, show me your hands.

We wrestle not against flesh and blood. But this war in my members. War between members. War all around. Came back home my mind wasn't sound. I hear voices. It's not God. Take that uniform off. Unloose those boots. Dog tags no use.

What happens when a soldier takes off his uniform and steps back into the civilian world. I've been to AA meetings. Seen a therapist too. Drinking problem. I don't get drunk, I get awesome. Take it to the head. What's going on in your head?

In the meeting the people are just like you. Ruth is there. Onesismus sits by Potifers wife. Go figure. She needs to be delivered. Bathsheba came smelling like good soap. Johnathan and his military ability giving good hope. Debra, She might judge me. Hagar, running from her problems. Abrahams baby mama. Ahothophel and Jobs wife, have to tell them to hush. Talk too much.

I was talking to my therapist. She said it's as if you are a beautiful two-story home. Why do you live in the basement? All my friends are there. I'm overlooked. Even with all my engagements.

Trying to ignore the trauma. Tripping over IEDs, I mean the past. Blinded by the war inside. Instead of building my house I've built walls filled with lies. Locking others out, I'm trapped inside. She said write your feelings down, so you can put your feelings down. Leave it in your devotion. The truth of God shall rule not your emotions.

Sanity is leaving my own thoughts deceiving me. Struggling with sin. In my own strength. Seeking to be independent of him. Controlled by my own desires. Carnal. All my thoughts are liars. Stunts my growth. Gods' weapons. Prayer, Faith, Hope.

Walk in the Spirit. Not in the flesh. My flesh wont rest. Jehovah Shalom. God that gives me peace, but these flashbacks come forth like the beast.

Rockets flying over my head so close I can feel the heat. Suicide bomber standing near, as a matter of fact ten feet. Why are you so calm? Because I know my father. No weapon formed shall prosper. But this fear I have yet to conquer.

Adonai, Master and lord, Teaching me my true sword. Not this 9mm on my hip, 50cal where I have a tight grip, 203 grenade launcher attached to my M4 America has come to adore.

Whole armor of God, full battle rattle, its heavy, Narrow path, trying to stay steady. Come here you They don't call you by your name. Back and forth with wars. Depression is a sore. Anxiety and adjustment disorder. PTSD is a trauma hoarder. No longer enjoy the things I use to. Emotions rearranged. Eating and sleeping habits changed. I'm not social. Ignore the call, relationships suffer. I struggle with being a lover.

I must go deep; pain is starting to leak. No longer continuing in sin. I can't stand to hear my husband weep. No more excuses I'll get to the root of it. Manipulating man. At the end of the day upon this rock. The rocks cried out. My heart had no place to stand. Emotionally unstable. Pain was never dealt with just rearranged. Felt like I had been crying for days. Tears were never shed. I was crying in other ways. Looking for man's approval. In their arms I could lie.

I would be comforted of my pain. Developing soul ties giving in to Satan's lies. Thinking love from a significant other would tell my pain that final goodbye. What I really wanted was the world.

To treat me like I deserve. I'm on the corner. They drive pass as if I have no honor. They don't like when I beg for money. I may be dirty, but I seek clean living among his clean linen.

My therapist makes me talk about my pain intoxicating her with who I blame. She can't even walk. My heart is blocked. Pride has her running into walls. Mentally frail, spiritually I smell. Jericho walls. Too much in me to be locked behind these gates. I need Rahab's grace.

Never state a problem without a solution. There is no substitution. Those gods I've bowed to, like Rahab's prostitution. Idolatry for the world. Alter I'm misusing. The truth shall make you free. He is true. He has made me but seeing through a glass darkly. Looking at myself. I just can't cope. My character is low. Inner me is bad news. Gospel, I didn't choose.

Substituting meditation for medication. Suicidal thoughts while taking this death walk. We die daily. Ye are not your own. Touch not my anointed. Contemplated suicide. That was something that I tried. Fell asleep standing up. The enemy sowed tares. No one cares. I can't sleep. I guess I'll take two, all of these.

I'm sick. Sick of love. Sometimes I wonder if this medicine even works. Same thing that helps me feel good makes me hurt. But I ignorantly indulge in this illness. The sweet bitter fulfillment. It drags me. I can no longer resist my resistance, so it has me. Like a drug in my vein. Not caring it causes pain. Addiction has taken place. Now I want my drug dealer to carry me through rehabs grace. Same thing I want more of makes me sick. If I resist it, I'm relapsing and repenting.

Trying to take it back to the beginning, when we first met. Hello, my name is, Love of the world. I will ponder your heart. You will forever mention me. I've been whirlwind twisting since infancy. I softly replied quickly. I'm sick of love. But in the midst of what I didn't see, oh how the world was so SICK. Of me.

My love for the world had me ill. Iron sharpens iron. My iron was low. With His blood I wasn't filled. Covered by the blood. I know His name. Using it in vain. Blood pumping through my veins was stained. SON of GOD standing in the midst of me bleeding out. I still have doubt. The devil put his taste in my mouth. Oh, taste and see. No bread and fish, just MRE's

Eyes straight ahead. Stuck on my past. I watched my six. Fighting demons of my history. Not the demons of my dependency. Praise the lord. Pass the ammunition. Little confession. Less repenting. Blood on my hands, friendly fire, Man down, but I stay fifteen minutes prior. Make a hole. I'm digging, I'm digging. I need good ground. He's coming back. I'm losing faith. Hurry up and wait.

I was built on confession of his lordship. A confessional body holding to the truth. But I got lost in the crowd. I'm not convicted. Oh, the sensation of religion. Too super of a man to trust the supernatural man. I'm in my feelings, five senses revealing. Touch, if I could touch the hem. Maybe I'll settle for him. Taste, your own vomit, I've returned. The smell is deadly, walk by faith not by sight, rarely. My ears are heavy.

Leaning to my own understanding. Voices in my head. I'm not one, SPLIT. ETC. ETC. With the mind we serve the Lord. Holy ground, my feet are covered. I got red socks. I got blue socks too. The mind of the church when God is not first. There's a crumb on your shirt.

The great I AM. I AM the Light of the world.

But me I am the church.

FEAR

 GOD

NOT

MAN

There's Power in Submission.

Sometimes you have to like lonely.

Being single can be a gift if not yet for you for Him.

But see I had this dream of having husband, career, nice home, and car, two kids, boy and girl.

That was going to be my world.

THE AMERICAN DREAM

Until God woke me up from my sleep

This world is NOT about me

He that is unmarried careth for the things that belong to the Lord. How he may please the lord

There's power in submission.

Be it unto me according to thy will.

That American dream he might tell you to be still.

Our goal is to keep company with Him.

Live a life of love and keep from sin.

To not love with caution signs

If He lives in us the love that spews out should be fully divine

Be careful not to allow love in a relationship to become lust.

But He fits and I just want to live Fitz and Liv SCANDLE when we waste life on things, we have to do in the dark.

When the light comes on you will see nothing, but shame don't be shocked.

Rip the covers off those frauds.

See how attractive they are in the light of your God!

Those secrets they tell you to keep make sure they benefit the king.

If you forget God in a relationship, He will forget you had a relationship and will not sustain it.

Never ignore you need the foundation of God to maintain it.

Relationships will not last if you keep doing them with memories of your past.

Mr. and Mrs. Perfect Do not exist.

If you can't be satisfied with just you and your savior don't think you and man alone can satisfy your nature

But I want my man with a body of a god.

If you're not married yet don't be shocked

That god may get in the way of your God, your blessing might be blocked.

36, 26, 36, Look at those hips

Hope your love is based off something a little more than this.

If you plan on getting old and having kids those hips will be missed

Getting to know the God in a person and mercy to know the person.

Let that be your bliss.

Goal to not let their light go dim.

If someone ever ask, are you ready to meet your maker? You can respond, I already know him.

To submit or not to submit

The story of my life, or maybe even a wife

Are you being the one to take a bite of that fruit that has no use?

Are you seeking God or seeking to be God in this marriage?

In God you seek to be used

But he that is married careth for the things of the world how he may please his wife.

Difference between loving and spoiling

Don't always give them their appetite.

Give them what they need.

Christ love wasn't cheap.

He didn't love to get something from us.

But to make us free

Loving your wife, you're doing yourself a favor.

God blesses that behavior.

Guard the man's heart submit it to God.

Then submit yourself to YOUR husband.

Stay in a position of prayer.

When it comes to church big mama shouldn't be the only one going there

Church is good.

Too much church can be misunderstood.

Sometimes you must come out the spirit to be a mother or a wife to that significant other.

Balance in everything

Leaning on consistency that is within

Because God lives within and doesn't change

If we are unstable creatures God is not to blame

Stay in good terms being held together by love.

Grace of Christ is the only good ground in life.

Submit all relationships to Christ.

NOURISH

OTHERS

WITH

GODS

TRUTH

Who

Invited

Grace?

God created heaven and earth, there was nobody.

In Christ Jesus, when he suffered, he did it alone. There was nobody.

Unto good works in need of the Holy Ghost, Mary checked the grave, there was NO BODY.

In the beginning God created, God moved, God said, God saw, God divided, God called.

Reflection of his glory, our lives, His story, but history will say, Adams way, would separate from love and grace.

He loves me, He loves me not. Love is patient, love is kind, love is ugly, love is muddy, love will get you dirty, it can be quite bloody.

Like a curse, they beat him as if they had power over him. He could have easily overpowered them.

The battle is over power. We wrestle not against flesh and blood.

Love God, Love your neighbor. But sin is where we cater.

Why does fruit taste so good when its forbidden? Gods wondering where I am. When I'm in sin I'm gone from him.

I loved sin so much, he became that, that's when YHWH turned his back, thirty pieces of silver, the cost of a slave, age thirty started ministry, thirty three got up from the grave.

Born of a virgin, when they saw him, they worshipped. See him for who he really is! Glory!

From the crown of his HEAD TO the sole of his FEET.

Crown of thorns on his HEAD, but you don't want your thorn in the FLESH. HAIR like wool, don't be a fool, Apple of his EYE, EARS given to hear, come here runaway bride, your husband is near. Lost in the world you've lost your identity, cheating with your first love, friend of the enemy. Remaining his foe. He was tied to a post, BACK exposed, gave his BACK to the smiters, CHEEKS to them that plucked his HAIR. Hid not his FACE from shame and spitting, see he is forgiving. Made heaven and earth by his great power and stretched out ARM. Unto us a child is born. HAND not too short that it cannot save, nail pierced HANDS. You don't have to see the grave. LEGS not broken; FEET pierced. My sheep can hear. Adams side opened for woman. Jesus side pierced for the church.

Talk about church hurt, weight of the body. CHURCH hung till suffocation. No man takes my life, I gave it for your sanctification. Blood drained, now blood stained, covered by his blood that remains. Sweat drops of blood, fell, jailed, stripped him, scarlet robe for sale, nailed, holding keys to death and hell, tore down the vail, Salvation! From the Father, through the Son, by the Spirit. Good works can't produce it, a product of it, so you don't become useless, disfigured clay, failing to seek his face.

WHO invited GRACE? Let her in to help you mend. Not worried about the world's rejection. With Grace there is an exception, in the belove is your reflection of greater works and his acceptance, As a sheep dependent on the shepherd's protection. Weary not in well doing. Seems like your enemy is pursuing. You don't have to hang Judas; Judas will hang himself. He's already in ruin. Walking in the light, your actions should reflect Christ.

Bring every work into judgment. Well done my good and faithful servant. Seek his FACE until you find his FEET.

Every KNEE!

THE

HEART

OF

THE

CHURCH

IS

THE

GOSPEL

SINNERS PERCEPTION

Therapy! for lay members, clergy, church members, and sinners.

Take me back to where church started birthing religion instead of Christians.

It seems to be a disconnect with the body and the head. Reading through the sixty-six. Were not on the same page. Not eating the same bread.

Leaning to our own understanding. Sheep wander when they wonder. Birthing bastard children with no honor for God. Use His name in vain. Issue of blood. Refusing His blood. Sickness in your vein its vain going to church this Sunday.

Get you a suit, they won't accept you unless you look like they do. Teach you to pretend to be something you're not fake and phony. Scared to be me I know you'll disown me. Easier to get along with the unsaved than the saved. Half the time they're truer than the saints. They say to proclaim Christ but they really aint. Supposed to be examples of Christ, I went to church and cried.

All I saw was strife. I didn't want to be like the examples I saw. I want my Christianity to be more than getting a car. Most unsaved don't like coming to church. They don't have the right clothes for the fashion shows. If you wear what you have, they consider you a hoe. Sit you on the back row. You don't feel welcomed. Might as well just go.

We don't respect God. We don't respect his people. Claiming to belong to God, Steady doing evil.

Coming to church trying to follow your leader, end up being deceived, find out they mislead you.

They only accept the righteous, God only accepts the sinners.

Looking to judge, instead of looking to the judge.

Not preaching the word, preach their own sermon. Wonder why the sinners don't budge.

You can't bring a sinner out of the closet if you're still stuck in one yourself. He's coming back for his rainbow. Stop acting like you hate them. He'll deal with that himself.

Only reason why you seek him, you want his wealth. Trying to be like the world loving it too. In gospel music, we do what they do.

The deeper we get in religion, the deeper the division. Its not about Jewish, catholic, or Muslim tradition but YHWH bring sinners to repentance.

What's the difference? Between a club and church that does not win souls. Too friendly don't want to offend the true gospel is not being told. Since when do we have to lower his standard to bring a sinner to repentance?

Sit in church looking at the world lusting what they got. The only envy we should have. They are sold out to their gods, and we are not.

Neglecting the truth, Anorexic in your faith, look big but your spirit man needs to be fed. Not with houses, cars, and clothes, The masters bread. On this bread you choke. Refusing to cast cares. Carry your own yoke.

God teaches us on His word we should stand. Not to fall in love with the devil's plan.

Finances. God wants you to pay your part. Ministries have become businesses. Taking two mites from the poor has become an art. Manipulating their need, with false hope, they can't see.

Making profits off prophets that gospel being preached Christ did not teach. Ten, twenty, can I get thirty. Instead of tithe and offering we're auctioning. Sitting here waiting for change, waiting for a change, when you shortchange God You make you change short.

The church is stuck on giving two bucks but want a million in return, a million is what you yearn, his work you haven't learned.

I outran Peter, I got there first. Finish the race. Stop being in competition with grace. Mary, running to the tomb, still looking for a body. Pastor, Pastor. Complaining about church hurt. Our church is hurt. Confidence in man, refusing to make Romans your romance. Man has failed you, now you focus on the wound, not the womb. That tomb was borrowed.

Salvation is not what you see its what you believe. It's hard to believe when you yourself have been deceived. Mind full of doubt, all the preachers tell you to do is shout.

Go to the alter, its just like getting lit. Instead of getting high, I get knocked out to cope with this. Addicted to the tradition so caught up in religion. We no longer conduct ourselves as Christians. Crackhead Christians is what we've become. Pastor the dope man we the baseheads, feigning for that crack to cope with this lack. Church is the new trap.

Get your check, throw it at the alter ten percent is all this hit cost you. We look like we seek God. Decorate it just right. Sundae salvation. We don't want desert we want dessert. I want this I don't want that. Choose your own salvation.

Go to church and pretend. Hide behind mask. Treat our preachers like strippers and throw them a little cash. Doing Gods work without Gods Spirit. Ignoring be ye transformed. In church but to this world we have conformed.

Moral compass interrupted. Blind beggar with more vision to believe. Upon this rock ill build my church but rocks cry out when wounded egos are hurt. Call out the called out. Desiring titles as if you're entitled. Seeking to be perfect Christians instead of seeking to be like Christ. You're your own idol.

Our vision is blurred. Focal point helps to align the body. Unity in YHWH, baptism, Spirit, love, hope, and faith.

Preaching a crooked gospel and expecting the saints to stay straight.

Develop a depth of understanding instead of struggling with the basics.

Desiring spiritual challenges instead of entertainment.

Enemy of offense keeps you from deliverance.

Serve HIM pass your five senses. Senses have limits, come up in the Spirit.

Seeing Him who is unseen. Christian's perception is the ability to see not be seen.

GOD

STILL

HEALS

Little Girl

I must go deep because the pain is starting to leak.

No longer continuing in sin because I can't stand to hear my father weep.

So, no more excuses ill get to the root of it.

Manipulating man but at the end of the day my heart had no place to stand.

Emotionally unstable

Pain was never dealt with just rearranged.

It felt like I had been crying for days.

Tears were never shed.

I was crying in other ways.

Looking for something

If I could just have that one relationship in their arms I could lay

I would be comforted of my pain.

Developing soul ties

Giving into Satans lies

Thinking love from another would tell my pain that finally goodbye.

But what I really wanted was my mother

To teach me and protect me.

As I grew up, she would always reject me.

Which would always upset me?

No affection I felt no acceptance.

Every time I would get close to her, she would push me away

Saying Meagan, I'm tired, telling me to go play.

So, I Played

Where the devil stayed

Turns out my best friend was only seven, but she was gay.

She taught me things my young mind wasn't ready to learn.

Wanting to be touched by love but got lust in return.

Now it burns.

Turned into frustration and pain.

Wanting things that has the devil's name.

Doing things in secret thinking that its hidden

Got the devils appetite.

But my mom, thinks everything is alright.

Instead of telling her all we do is just fight.

She's telling me she's been a good mother.

Asking me what's wrong.

Its too late now

You waited too long.

What's in me now holds me strong.

Knowing the devil put it there and it doesn't belong.

Friends asking me, why do you smoke the way you do?

And when you have problems, when is liquor what you turn too.

Wondering why I hate women the way I do.

I wasn't taught how to love them.

So, lust is what I used.

People use to call me little girl.

I never really liked it.

There was a little girl in me I always had to fight with

Fear of raising a little girl not knowing how to teach.

How to be the women God raises and not that little girl that was in me

That little girl in me that always wanted to be.

But she hid behind shyness and timidness.

You see that little girl that looks in the mirror and doesn't like what she sees.

So, she tries to be like that woman on tv and not what God created her to be which is Adams help meet.

Little girl I know you hear me fighting all these tears for all these years.

I'm talking to you.

The one that's trying to ignore me.

Yeah you, God is not through.

When it comes to your womanhood you think you blew because the devil tried to confuse it

Making you lean on emotions and the things you've been through.

When it comes to your womanhood to give you a cloudy view

Little girl I'm talking to you.

The devils plan only works when you allow it to

Maybe I must go a little deeper.

Go visit that tomb stone where you stopped living.

Decided to love your lust and continue sinning.

The devil meant it for evil, but Jesus came so you too can be free.

Little girl there's a woman in you that you have yet to conceive.

Leaning on what the devil gave you.

Not what God told you to believe

Therefore, you don't seek for other men but that woman you thought you should be.

Little girl I'm talking to you, that little girl that was just like me.

Jesus came so you too can be free.

Freedom doesn't come with an ease.

You must want it.

It's something you have to receive.

Little girl

BREAK FREE

www.ingramcontent.com/pod-product-compliance
Lightning Source LLC
LaVergne TN
LVHW051747080426
835511LV00018B/3252